After Goliath

After Goliath

Sketches and dialogues
that communicate the message

JANET EASTWOOD

kevin
mayhew

First published in 2003 by
KEVIN MAYHEW LTD
Buxhall, Stowmarket, Suffolk, 1P14 3BW
E-mail: info@kevinmayhewltd.com

KINGSGATE PUBLISHING INC
1000 Pannell Street, Suite G, Columbia, MO 65201
E-mail: sales@kingsgatepublishing.com

9 8 7 6 5 4 3 2 1 0

ISBN 1 84417 071 3
Catalogue Number 1500587

Cover design by Jonathan Stroulger
Edited by James Croft
Typesetting by Louise Selfe
Printed in Great Britain

Contents

About the author

Janet Eastwood is an experienced parish priest and minister of the gospel. As a priest she is rooted in the life of her urban parish. As a minister she is determined to tell the gospel in ways that make people sit up, lean forward, laugh and learn, and even feel a tear welling up in the corner of the eye.

St Paul told us that we see truth through an opaque glass. That's how it's been translated. He actually wrote that we see through the glass in stories. This was the method of Jesus. He told stories not for children but for audiences of adults and children together. The parables are for all ages.

The parables of Jesus surprised and entertained his followers. They lost themselves in the stories and then, often with the twist in the tale, were jolted into seeing themselves. Dramatic stories have the power to touch the heart as well as the mind. They can make you think and feel. They can pose questions that touch your emotions.

Janet has, out of the wealth of her parish experience, set down these sketches in the hope that with her you too might find new ways of exploring familiar truths.

The Rt Revd James Jones
Bishop of Liverpool
31 January 2003

Introduction

Jesus was a fantastic raconteur. In a land and an age where people loved telling stories, and were used to listening, he held their attention, and tens and hundreds and thousands flocked to hear him tell parables and to preach. Stories were life and breath to his followers.

I have been fortunate in all the churches in which I have grown and worked to have been provided with many opportunities to tell stories, usually in the form of drama.

It started when I was a young adult and was given the chance to write a script (which has long disappeared) weaving together music readings and drama to recount the story of the crucifixion and resurrection for an Easter Sunday evening service.

Ainsdale, St John, in the Diocese of Liverpool was the first church in which I worked as a stipendiary minster, and I was privileged to work with some of the best youth workers in the area, one of whom loved drama. He introduced me to narrators, choral speaking and mime and his boundless enthusiasm meant that every child and teenager in the church was desperate to be involved. Two other leaders showed me how mime on its own can bring people to tears and laughter, and with these three principally involved, all things dramatic began to find a home in St John's liturgy – and not all were confined to family worship. They strayed into other services as well.

My next home was in Kirkby Lonsdale, where, if we did not have the large numbers of young people to work with as in my previous church, we certainly had enthusiasm, and one of my fondest memories is of a service based on the story of Jonah and the whale. I had been asked if the youth leaders and teenagers could make a whale, and of course I was delighted. I simply didn't expect that such gargantuan proportions could be reached by wire and papier-mâché as I looked up to see an eight-foot-long whale lilting its way down the aisle on eight legs poking out from beneath its massive body.

Then I came back to Liverpool and to Holy Trinity, Wavertree, to a church that, over the last 50 years at least has had a drama group of some form running. Currently it is a youth drama group, but previously it has been an adult one, and so in my current spiritual home are natural actors and of course this being Liverpool, one or two drama queens to boot! It was here, in a church with excellent acoustics, clear lines of vision from most places in the body of the church, and a great capacity to absorb, and enjoy, different ways of worshipping and communicating the gospel, that lots of things came together and drama became, not just a bit of the service, but a part of the liturgy.

I didn't know where to turn at first, there was so much talent just waiting to be harnessed. Now, through stories and dialogues, narrations and mime, as well as straightforward drama, we try to share our faith within and beyond church services. The leaders of the Youth Drama Group work hard with our young people, but some members of the original drama group continue to provide expertise and inspiration through their own experience, and it is always good to see all ages – not just youth – participating.

We always try very hard not to simply slot things in, but to look at the services as a whole – the prayers, readings, hymns and songs all working with the drama to form a cohesive unity of worship.

Music is a vital component and our organist and I regularly sit down with the script for a service and work through the draft, making sure that words, music and silences are in harmony.

What follows are some of the resources that have been used over the years in all these churches, but especially in Holy Trinity. With these also are some brand new ones.

They are there to help you and inspire you – not to be followed slavishly. You will see that most involve a narrator or two. This works well for us. We use the lectern and the pulpit – both with microphones – and choose clear, experienced speakers. This means we can include others not so confident in the knowledge that the story will still go on even if the smaller voices aren't as clear. Generally, these smaller voices grow into bigger, more confident voices.

These sketches are made to be tweaked – and may well be better for your church if you do so. You might like to adapt them to make a complete drama, or have the narrators do all the talking and the actors simply performing the actions. A few of the stories have a definite bias towards the city in which our church lives and grows. I make no apologies for this! Liverpool is a part of our lives, but do change the details to fit in with your town, community or current situation.

Finally, all this provides enjoyment and entertainment in the practising and the producing, but our chief aim throughout all our worship and work is to learn more about the love of God and to share it. Through the humour we want to make people think and to question long-held ideas and prejudices. Through a straightforward retelling of a familiar story, we want to remind people of the love Christ has for them. Through the way in which the service is conducted, to which the drama and the congregation are integral, we want people to feel the Spirit moving and inspiring them.

Janet Eastwood, July 2002

PART ONE

Sketches on Contemporary Issues

Beckham's foot

In the Spring of 2002, football fever reached the dizzy heights when we heard that David Beckham, the English Captain, had been injured and a bone in his foot had been broken. He had just six weeks to hope and pray that it healed in time for him to captain England in the FIFA World Cup in Japan. The media and all his fans had just six weeks to do something about it. The media excelled themselves! Pictures of Beckham's foot adorned virtually every newspaper, the opinions of medics and physiotherapists were earnestly sought and even Uri Geller (of fork-bending fame) was brought on television to exhort the nation to pray.

That same week, the news carried reports of the conflict in Afghanistan, the Sangatte asylum-seekers camp in France, and developments in the political scene in Burma – a country which has suffered decades of civil war and the abuse of human rights. These were all submerged in the erupting frenzy over Beckham's foot – which did play in the World Cup. Did the prayer help? Was as much prayer offered for these other situations? If not, why not?

It reminded me of a story I once read: a snow storm had come to the forest, and all the birds and animals sheltered, but the robin and the dove both watched the flakes fall and settle on the branches of a tree.

'How much does a snow flake weigh?' the robin asked the dove. 'Less than nothing,' she replied. The snow continued to fall and the branches of the tree began to sag under the weight of the snow. The robin repeated his question, 'How much does a snow flake weigh?' and the dove replied, 'One snowflake weighs less than nothing, and on its own can do nothing. Many flakes are so heavy they can change the shape of a tree.'

A   One thousand, four hundred and seventy-two took part in the FIFA 2002 World Cup.

B   One thousand, four hundred and seventy-two converged on Japan and Korea to practise and prepare . . .

A   and many wondered and worried about the outcome.

B   One thousand, four hundred and seventy-two were coached, shod and sent out onto the pitch to run and play and, we hoped, to win.

A   But one was special.

B   One was cherished and coddled.

A   Just one out of one thousand, four hundred and seventy-two caught the media's attention.

B   Just one struck fear into the hearts of millions.

A   Just one was prayed for – David Beckham.

B   Beckham's foot!

A   The only podiatric extremity in history to achieve fame in such a way –

B   and all because one little bone was trodden on . . .

A   and broken.

B   GMTV invited Uri Geller to exert his influence over the injured appendage. And we in turn were asked to place our hands on a cartoon foot on the television screen . . .

A   and pray.

B   It was almost a reason for national mourning when Beckham's foot –

A   his right foot, his best kicking foot –

B   was injured in a football tackle,

A   was x-rayed by doctors, photographed by paparazzi,

B   and written about by respected journalists.

A   Beckham's foot

B   had more news coverage than the escalating fighting in Afghanistan;

A   more newspaper columns than Aung San Suu Kyi, leader of the National League for Democracy in Burma, who was released from prison after 19 months of house arrest;

B and was photographed more than the people in the Sangatte asylum-seekers camp in France.

A Beckham's foot

B had more media coverage than anything else that week.

A Tony Blair's cabinet talked about it,

B the Queen sent it a 'get well' card,

A a special boot was made to protect it should it be fit to play . . .

B and finally, prayers were answered, and Beckham's foot got to play in the World Cup.

A Sadly, Beckham's general fitness had also suffered through his foot's injury

B and the first match was lost.

A Though the second one was won.

B But they didn't get through to the final.
Perhaps if we'd prayed about his health as well as his foot . . .

A and about the war in Afghanistan,
the asylum seekers in Sangatte,
human rights in Burma,
and *all* the English football team . . .

B Beckham might have fared better in the World Cup,

A and so might the England team,
the soldiers and civilians,
the asylum seekers,
and the Burmese people.

B If we'd prayed –

A such a small thing, Beckham's foot, and easy to pray about;

B such a big thing, Afghanistan,

A too large to contemplate;

B such a distant thing, Burma,

A too complicated to learn about;

B such an angry state of affairs, Sangatte;

A we don't want to pray about that.

B But Beckham's foot . . .

A well, that's a different thing entirely.

B But if we had prayed,

A like we did for Beckham's foot,

B who knows what might have happened?

A Faith too can be such a small thing; Jesus said it can be as small as a mustard seed, which is tiny, and yet still grows into a great plant.

B Beckham's foot was small, but a whole team depended on it.

A I wonder just how many depend on our prayers?

Big Brother

Big Brother has enjoyed phenomenal success in the genre of 'reality TV'. Its name is taken from the phrase coined by George Orwell in his book, 1984, which prophesied a time when constant surveillance would become a way of life, though hated by some.

The author, Ben Elton, has recently written a novel inspired by the cult TV programme. In Dead Famous *a group of young adults is brought together under the ever-watchful eye of Peeping Tom, but excitement turns to horror when a murder is committed – and Peeping Tom and his 30 cameras fail to pinpoint the murderer.*

This sketch was inspired by recent media interest and criticism of Big Brother *and the 'cult of celebrity' it whips up, plus Ben Elton's provocative book. It's a sketch with three acts, which can be run one after the other, or punctuated with appropriate prayers and readings as part of a service.*

ACT 1

Jamie I'd love to go on *Big Brother*. Imagine all the money you could make –

Cass And all the privacy you'd lose.

Jamie But we'd be famous –

Cass Or notorious. Just think of that poor girl last time who was likened to a pig.

Jamie Well maybe she –

Cass Don't even think it! How would you like your personality to be exposed, dissected, analysed by millions?

Jamie I've got nothing to hide. Lots to show in fact *(strutting, showing off his physique)* – six pack, good pecs – *Big Brother* could well like me, and I'd like the money!

Cass But only one person will win, and you have to spend 10 weeks – 10 whole weeks – banged up with strangers and cameras everywhere, a disembodied voice telling you what to do and creating unreal situations. They even have a psychotherapist to hand if it sends you off the rails!

Jamie But *Big Brother* looks after you – there's food, things to talk about and things to do . . . and even that psychotherapist has your well-being at heart. Just think about it: you don't have to pay bills or anything like that while you're in there; you make mates with the others –

Cass And at the same time you're nominating them to be voted off! I don't think so!

Jamie But at the same time, people see you, you get famous, and even if you don't win, the papers might pay you for your story . . .

Cass But why should they do that when they've seen you being foolish on TV, been bored by inane conversation and amateur psycho-speak?

Jamie You just won't give it a chance, will you? *Big Brother* could be good to us, teach us about ourselves, give us a new start in life? And that can't be bad . . . Can it?

You can pause here to reflect on the choices that lay before Jamie and Cass, and the way in which their life is affected by outside forces and the media and internet in particular. This could lead to either prayers of thanksgiving for the ways in which information is relayed and/or confession for the ways in which it is used negatively to influence individuals and pervade the society in which we live.

ACT 2

Anna Why don't you come to Jake's party with me? It'll be wicked – ev'ryone'll be there, and his parents are away. Booze, women for you, music, dope –

Tim That's all you think about, isn't it – parties and drinking, sex and getting stoned.

Anna *(Shrugging her shoulders)* Doesn't everyone? *(Cajoling)* Come with me, it'll be a laugh. Anyway, you like parties!

Tim Sure, I'll take you, you'll get off with someone, drink too much, get sick, then I'll take you home and it'll be a real laugh. I don't think so! Besides, I've got something better to do –

Anna Oh, for God's sake –

Tim Precisely.

Anna What does that mean?

Tim It means I'm going to hear someone talk about God.

Anna I don't believe it! *The* party of the year, and you're going to hear someone talk about . . . *God*?

Tim Yes.

Anna *(After a short pause, then laughing a bit uncertainly)* That is so like you! Winding me up like that. God indeed! Come on, you've got to get ready *(attempting to pull him away)*.

Tim No, I'm serious. There's a series of talks down at the Cathedral about the Ten Commandments, and they're really good. I want to go back.

Anna *(Incredulously)* Really good? The Ten Commandments?

Tim *(Nods his head)* Come with me. Please. It's not like you imagine; there's music and laughter and the talks are excellent; I under-stand what the guy's talking about, he really makes sense . . .

Anna I don't think so. Don't do this, don't do that, don't have fun and on top of all that, those super-sincere Christians, with their plas-tic smiles and knowing looks, criticising our clothes, our music, our fun. Ten Commandments? Sounds more like George Orwell and Big Brother to me.

Pause here to consider what people on the outside of Christianity think about what goes on inside our faith. Is it all restrictions and going to church on Sundays? How would you change Anna's perceptions of a church which has no relevance to her life?

Think about using a Bible reading, perhaps 2 Corinthians 6:3-10 if you want to address regular members of a congregation, or Luke 15:11-end, if the service is welcoming people who are new to the church: the Prodigal

Son (some call it the tale of the Loving Father) is always good to tell people of the love of God. There could well be another reading that is just right for your congregation.

This prayer, based on one written by St Augustine, could be appropriate:

Almighty God,
you have made us for yourself,
and our hearts are restless
till they find their rest in you.
Teach us to offer ourselves to your service,
that here we may have your peace,
and in the world to come may see you face to face;
through Jesus Christ our Lord. Amen

Alternative Service Book

ACT 3

Mark It was an amazing time – it's still hard for me to put into words all I saw and felt, and to explain the significance of it all. To Uncle Peter and the others, he was a dear friend, a leader, but to me then, a teenager, he was the Big Brother I never had.

Peter encouraged me to go with them and listen to him. I would listen to the adults talking about the things he said, trying to make sense of it all; but they were so busy hearing his words, they forgot the looking and seeing!

They didn't see the glint in his eye if he told an improbable story, or the smile that split his face when he caught a child up in his arms and swung her onto his shoulders.

They didn't seem to see the tears that streamed down his face when the sisters told him Lazarus was dead, and the anger when people tried to trick him into not healing on the Sabbath.

Instead, they dissected Jesus' words and analysed them. The disciples did it to understand him and the priests and lawyers did it to catch him out. And they missed the essence of the man: the joy of his living and the exultation of his loving; the sadness which dragged him down, and the anger that spurred him on.

Some saw it and understood. Uncle Peter did – when he finally stopped reacting and started seeing and listening. John certainly did, but he's a deep one, rarely opening his mouth unless it's to say something significant.

Jesus loved him, that's for sure. There was a special bond there – just like brothers have. After all, on that terrible day it was John he asked to look after his mother.

But he was like that, looking out for other people all the time, taking on those he thought were bullies, or didn't know the truth, and making unbelievable sacrifices for them.

The night he was arrested, I was there. I saw Judas come and kiss Jesus, and I saw the guards surround him. I saw the fighting and I saw Peter take out his sword and swing it round, cutting off the ear of one of the soldiers.

I ran and hid for the noise was dreadful, and the fighting angry. My loincloth caught on a branch and I didn't dare go back for it. Finally, my heart pounding and my breath coming in great gasping sobs, I had to stop and look back.

Jesus had stopped the fighting. He stretched out his hand to the injured man . . . and his ear was restored! I saw it happen.

The next few days passed in a daze. Peter and the others kept a low profile whilst Jesus went on trial. I was too young to under-stand why or even how it had happened, but the fact was that some people hated him and wanted him dead. It was bound to happen.

And so it was, one dark and evil day, that Jesus was taken outside the city walls, and crucified. *(Pause)*

We did not, could not, know that his death was not the end of his life, but the beginning of new life for the rest of us. We only began to realise days and weeks later not just the cost of his sacrifice but the rewards he won for us.

Jesus, my brother, my Big Brother, dying to save us all.

Consider singing or saying a version of the Creed. Follow this up with a brief address explaining the importance of Christ's death and resurrection, and lead into sharing the Peace.

Computella:
a modern fairy tale

Drudgery comes in many shapes and forms. For Cinderella, it was being permanently attached to a broom handle and sweeping the kitchens out, for Aladdin it was slaving for his wicked uncle, and for Computella it was being chained to a low paid job sat in front of a computer all day. Though their situations were different, they all shared certain similarities: a tyrant of a boss and a boring, boring job. The first two had a mythical, magical creature to provide a happy ending. Computella, however, lives in the real wide web-world where fairy tales don't have such predictable endings . . .

Use this modern fairy tale in a service to focus on hopes and dreams and disappointments too. Weave activities, songs and prayers through the three-part drama to draw the congregation into prayer.

Give each member of the congregation a sheet of paper with two headings written on it: 'I wish . . .' and 'My prayer is . . .'

PART 1

A   Computella was where she always was: sat in front of her computer.

B   Her name was really Chloe, but because no one ever saw her away from her computer, or spoke to her without hearing the keyboard keys clattering, Chloe became . . . Computella.

A   From early morning to long after dusk had fallen and the moon risen, she was there at the family business, answering the phone, dealing with angry clients, sorting out difficult suppliers, and sifting through hundreds of e-mails a day. The work never ended, it only grew.

B   The business had been started by her father, but after his divorce a new partner had been brought in to run the place. Computella, who had loved the film *101 Dalmations*, called her Cruella, and the partner in turn brought her two indispensable helpers with her – Crystal, the Human Resources Manager and Crispin, the Customer Services Manager.

A   It didn't help that Crystal had only one human resource to manage and that Crispin had only one customer service clerk to direct – and that they both bore the same name and worked at the same computer, and lived in the same body –

B   Yes, you've got it! Crystal and Crispin relied on Computella, not only to do her own work, of which there was more than enough, but they also expected her to do all theirs as well.

A   And so Cruella cracked the whip, Crispin and Crystal gave the orders, and Computella could never get anything right.

B   One night, when they had all gone home, she sat looking at her screen with sightless eyes. The others were all going to the premiere of a new film, and she'd been left to do the late shift: answering the phone to customers with problems.

A   And being honest, as Computella glanced at her reflection she wasn't sorry to be left behind. It didn't matter that she'd miss seeing Brad Pitt and Johnny Depp; they would only see this washed out, lank-haired, spotty, exhausted creature that stared back at her.

B   Then, over the speaker came the familiar tune announcing an e-mail. She thought of ignoring it, but habit got the better of her.

A   'You too can go to the premiere!' it said, and that was all it said.

B   Confused, she read the words again, this time out loud: 'You too can go to the premiere.'

A   'That's what I said, Chloe!' appeared on the screen.

B   Computella rubbed her eyes in disbelief – the computer was acting as if she had entered a chat room, and she hadn't. It called her Chloe – a name she had almost forgotten – and more than that, it answered her thoughts.

A   This time, Computella . . . Chloe spoke out loud. 'I *can* go to the premiere?'

B   'That's right. I have the power to grant three wishes. I have access to money, to clothes, to any resources you need. But just one word of warning – don't waste them. You can go to the premiere, or on holiday, or you can consolidate the finance I can provide in a series of wise investments. The world's your oyster, Chloe. Now I must go for a while.'

A 'But who are you?' Chloe cried, thoroughly confused.

B 'I'm the Computer Fairy,' wrote the computer, gaily. 'Good-bye!' *(Said like Anne Robinson)*

A And with that, the screen went blank, then writing reappeared:
Wish No. 1   Wish No. 2   Wish No. 3

B And the cursor flashed by *Wish No. 1* indicating that she should write her response . . .

After part 1

You have a sheet of paper in front of you with two headings.

The first says simply: *I wish . . .*

Write or draw something that you wish for yourself. It could be something you want to be when you grow up, or something you want to happen now. If you are grown up, it may be a change of job or situation.

Just one thing: don't put your name on the sheet, but write your age in the top corner. Keep it safe – you'll need it again.

Pause to write and then to sing 'Blessed be the name of the Lord' or some-thing similar.

PART 2

A There was no contest. Chloe had three wishes, her exhaustion had vanished, and she really did want to go to the premiere.

B Quickly, she typed into the space by *Wish No. 1* – 'I do want to go . . .',

A but then she stopped and deleted it, and then sat looking thought-fully at the computer screen.

B   Chloe did want to go to the premiere, but there was no need to waste a wish. She had the ticket – it was just that the others had piled up so much work that she had not even thought of using it.

A   She started to type again: 'Make me look . . .'

B   and again she stopped. She had been on the verge of saying, 'Make me look beautiful' and then she remembered that shops and hairdressers were all still open for another hour or two. Reason also played a part. She could get her hair and make-up done, that was easy, but time-consuming. Should she wish for the ultimate dress?

A   No. Crystal had brought two into work that morning, and could, of course, only wear one. Chloe tried it on and it fitted perfectly.

B   She ran happily into the hairdresser's next door and, caught up in her enthusiasm, they washed and dried her hair, stroked extra length into her eyelashes and coloured her lips red.

A   Chloe ran back to her office, slipped the dress over her shoulders and glanced in the mirror.

B   She looked a million dollars. Turning quickly to call a taxi, she lifted her skirts . . .

A   and to her horror saw, not delicate shoes,

B   but practical Doc Martens. And they would not do for a film premiere and Brad Pitt.

A   She nearly wept; but then she remembered the three wishes.

B   Turning the computer back on, there they were. She took a deep breath and quickly typed: 'a pair of shoes to go with this dress.'

A   She didn't breathe again for many seconds, as a wicked pair of desperately high-heeled, rhinestone-embellished, feather-flirting, shocking pink shoes appeared on the screen.

B   She wanted them.

A   She loved them.

B   She simply had to have them. And then somehow, miraculously, they left the screen and appeared on her desk.

A   And so she put them on.

B   No, she *tried* to put them on, but her feet were just that bit too big.

A   But Chloe was determined, and she squeezed her poor feet into the outrageously gorgeous shoes.

B   And promptly fell over and twisted her ankle.

After part 2

Sometimes we want something so badly – and then it goes wrong. It might be the perfect pair of shoes, but it could be something much more serious. And sometimes it's because we've been greedy or selfish as individuals, or even as countries, that bad things happen.

But Jesus promises a brand new beginning when we tell him how sorry we are for the wrong things we have done, so as you sit or kneel, let us ask God's forgiveness now.

Confession and absolution.

PART 3

A   So there was the first wish used up.

B   Was she happy? Not a bit.

A   She was angry, her foot hurt, and she simply couldn't get the wretched shoe off without hurting her poor ankle. There was nothing else for it. With tears of frustration and pain in her eyes, Chloe cut the slender ankle strap that was causing her such pain.

B   The relief was not instant and it was tempered by the new pain caused by the blood rushing back into her foot.

A   Slowly and painfully she hauled herself back onto her chair and looked again at the screen winking impassively at her.

B   The cursor was bobbing impertinently by the second wish.

A   How should she use this wish as the first had gone so disastrously wrong? She could wish for an ambulance – but one phone call could solve that problem – or she could even get a taxi to the hospital.

B   She could wish herself back in time before her ankle got hurt – but would she forget the sequence of events and simply relive them? With one wish gone, she wasn't prepared to gamble the second one.

A   Or was she? Chloe quickly scrolled the e-mail back and reread the computer's suggestion about investing money provided by the computer fairy.

B   With no more thought, she asked for £100,000 to be provided and promptly put it all into a dot.com company.

A   It took seconds to acquire the money . . .

B   seconds to invest it . . .

A   and seconds to see the dot.com company floated and sink without trace.

B   In less than two minutes she was back where she was – no, worse than she was, for now there was only one wish left.

A   Angrily, she shouted at the computer.

B   I wish I'd never seen you! I wish I'd never wished on you! Talk about the weakest link!

A   And a cheery little message was typed on the screen by an icon with short red hair –

B   Good-bye!

A   And as the screen faded, Computella . . . Chloe was left wondering whether it had all happened, or whether it had all been just a dream.

After part 3

Wishes don't always work. We can sit and dream, but sometimes we have to work for dreams to become reality and, more importantly, to pray.

Jesus said: 'Ask your Father in heaven for anything, and he will give it to you in my name.'

Later in the service, we will say our prayers, but today we want you to make the prayers. The second heading on your sheet of paper is about prayer. Stop and think for a moment, and then write. You will all know of at least one person who needs our prayers today, but consider for a moment larger groups of people or even countries whom we need to remember in our prayers today. Can you tell me some of them . . .?

Now choose just one and write it down. Then during the next song, pass them to the centre aisle, and the stewards will collect them in . . .

Sing: Seek ye first the kingdom of God
Readings: Psalm 37:1-7a; Luke 12:22-31

ADDRESS OUTLINE AND PRAYERS

Dreams are important. Sometimes they fizzle and die – but sometimes they become reality. My best friend knew when she was nine years old that she wanted to be a doctor – and she is.

*Sarah, who is 18, wants to work in research, finding cures for diseases such as cancer. Fiona has applied to Cambridge University but doesn't know if she'll get good enough grades at A level to realise her dreams. Julie, who is 17, dreams of backpacking in Australia. It will help her to be independent and learn about decision-making. Not only that, she'll see different people and a different country and, I hope, enjoy herself . . .

* *These are the dreams of young people in our congregation – substitute dreams that your own teenagers have.*

The readings remind us to wait on God and to listen to his voice – they are telling us to pray. The psalm also reminds us that if we delight in God, the desires of our hearts will agree with the plans he has for us. Take time, not only to dream, but also to think, plan and pray and listen to God. Some of our teenagers and young people have dreamed dreams . . . prayer might make them possible.

Older people have different dreams: *Jan wants security in her retirement;

Jim wants to see his grandchildren in Australia; Chris wants to get back to work after looking after her children for a few years; and Andrew wants a holiday to remember but has no money to pay for it!

*Again, use the hopes and dreams of your own folk.

They might not be as impossible as you think. Prayer focuses our minds, but much more than that, it allows God to work in us and through us. Now let us pray about the issues important to you.

Take some of the slips with dreams and prayers and read them out. You might like to have someone sorting through them during the address and picking out half a dozen different ones.

Judy's dream

I recently attended a church in York. During the service Judy Homer stood up to talk about her work with the mission agency, World Horizons, which tries to place Christians in situations that are literally on the horizons of the world in which missionaries work. The work they do is truly on the coalface as they seek to share their faith where Christians have rarely, if ever, been before.

For family reasons, Judy and her husband Alan have returned to Britain to work with the charity from its headquarters in Llanelli. Their family have been struggling with problems of illness and so when Judy shared, not only the work of World Horizons and her family situation, but also a dream which had given her great inspiration, we in the congregation were also inspired. Below is a dramatised reading reflecting on her dream.

It is presented as a dialogue, but it could just as easily be a reading for one voice introducing a service or sermon which focuses on the need to share the gospel wherever we are.

A Jesus is God and man, a concept almost too hard to understand.

B Yet it was because God loved the world so much that he sent Jesus; not to condemn the world, but that the world through him might be saved.

A St Paul encouraged the people of Philippi to have the mind of Jesus; to do nothing of self-interest and ambition; and to look always to the needs of others. He wrote:

B 'Jesus, who although he was in the same form as God,
did not regard equality with God as something to be exploited,
emptied himself, taking the form of a slave,

A was born in human likeness,
and as a human he humbled himself . . .' (Philippians 2:6-8a)

(Pause)

B I had a dream . . .

A I stood on a beach talking with my friend.

B   We were engrossed in each other,

A   enjoying the sunlight warming us

B   and the sand beneath our feet.

A   Then, without warning, a man sprinted between us,

B   startling us,

A   surprising us,

B   knocking us apart with his urgency.

A   He ran so fast I can still feel the wind he created whispering on my cheek.

B   We stopped talking and looked after the man rushing towards the seashore.

A   As he drew closer to the sea, he started stripping off his clothes, just throwing them onto the sands.

B   We ran after him, stopping for a moment to look at his clothes, flung so heedlessly onto the sand.

A   We looked at them and we picked them up. They were beautiful: silky to touch and richly embroidered. We had seen nothing like them before.

B   We held up the garment and in fine stitches saw the legend: King of kings and Lord of lords.

A   For a moment we were distracted, wondering what this could mean.

B   Then there was a noise – a shout!

A   Freed from his clothes, the man had plunged into the sea and was swimming out, out to the horizon,

B   and when we lifted our eyes, we saw what we should have seen and heard earlier:

A a voice shouting and arms waving in the distance –

B We should have heard them earlier but we were talking –

A growing fainter –

B we should have seen them earlier but we were absorbed in one another –

A at last he reached them, held them and rescued them,

B and we realised he'd rescued us as well.

(Pause)

A I can still feel the wind whispering against my cheek as he ran past.

B 'For the Son of Man came, not to condemn the world,
but in order that the world might be saved through him' (John 3:17).

A Thanks be to God.

Christ's fool

We have a tradition at Holy Trinity, grown over many years, of producing a drama for Advent which, though it is enjoyed by children, also carries a message for older people as well.

One of our favourites is Tolstoy's Little Shoemaker, *but there is a limit to the number of times this delightful play can be repeated. So, Bill Jones, a one-time member of the original drama group at Holy Trinity, was persuaded to come up with an alternative.*

The inspiration came, not just from Tolstoy, but also from a jester's out-fit made for one of the children at Holy Trinity for a children's fancy dress competition. There was a tunic quartered in wonderful red and blue velvet, but the crowning glory was a three-horned hat with jingle bells. It would have been a sin not to use it!

Fortunately, there was also a lithe and slim woman with a head that could just about squeeze into the hat and who was prepared to caper. We had our jester!

Narrator 1 It was a cold clear day – a bleak day if you were lonely or despairing. Christmas was only a day away and the commercial premises – the shops, the offices, the factories (those still in business, that is) – were bright with Christmas trees and decorations.

There was a pleasant air of anticipation in these places: the prospect of bumper sales for the shopkeepers; the factory workers' pleasure at big orders taking all their stocks; and the shoppers' frenzied spending.

All of them were looking forward to a holiday and a few days' gastronomic indulgence.

The churches were also decorated for their celebration of Christ's birth; devout Christians were warm and cosy in their fellowship and worship; but other people were also out and about on that day . . .

Some were Christians, some were not. Some looked poor and others were poor in their relationship with others.

Some were hungry and some had been so badly treated that many of these had no reason to celebrate, nor cause for delightful anticipation, for nothing good ever came to them or from them.

Narrator 2 Into this cold and dreary day came an ornate and bizarre figure, who danced and capered in a most eccentric manner.

The jester comes in to the back of the church, jingling his (or her) bells and dancing his way down the aisle, his pockets full of sweets to be given and thrown to the people. He moves down the central aisle or among the people and stops in different places to speak his lines.

He would have been grotesque if it were not for his bright clothes and the sheer vitality and humour that radiated from him. It was impossible to ignore the jester.

From the bells jingling on his upturned, pointed slippers to those tinkling on his three-horned blue and red hat, there was a vibrancy and life which made people turn their heads and smile at this figure of fun who was so in tune with their world.

Narrator 1 The jester danced his way to a group of children who huddled against the cold, like people old enough to be their grand-parents, then he said to them:

Jester Can you dance like me? I bet you can't . . .

Narrator 1 And he teased and cajoled them into dancing and playing with him. Before long, the children had forgotten the cold and the air was alive with their giggles and shrieks of laughter.

Throwing sweets to them all, the jester waved and danced away, the bells on his toes and hat proclaiming his journey as he smiled and waved and chatted to everyone he met on the way.

Even those deep into the darkest depression felt a fleeting lifting of their misery, as they saw – and felt – the jester's zest for life. They saw someone who appeared content with his lot – and in the main they were right.

Narrator 2   But there was just one thing the jester longed for with all his heart. He knew that he was blessed by many good things: humour, health, happiness, but there was something for which his heart yearned, one thing to complete his joy.

Narrator 1   He wanted to see Christ, and on the eve of his Lord's nativity, if he could see Christ, the jester would want nothing else.

Narrator 2   And so as he danced and laughed, he prayed to God whom he had worshipped all his life,

Jester   To see you Lord is all I ask.

Narrator 1   And then it seemed to him that a quiet voice spoke to him:

Christ   Before this day is ended, you will see me.

Narrator 2   The jester shook his head, bewildered, and set his bells jingling.

Jester   I must be dreaming – I'm only a fool. There are many more deserving, needing people; they will see Christ before me.

Narrator 1   And so he danced on his way, pondering the words he had heard, so that he almost fell over a pile of old rags. But they weren't rags, and the pile moved as an old man raised his arms to protect his head.

Narrator 2   The jester knelt down immediately.

Jester   I'm so sorry, I didn't see you.

Narrator 2   Then he dug deep into his pockets and found some money.

Jester   Come, my friend, let's find you some food and warmth for the night.

Narrator 2   There was a shelter nearby, and the jester saw the old man welcomed into the warmth.

He walked on until he came to a church, the stained glass windows glowing with the light of a hundred candles. He heard choristers singing and peeped inside as a long procession of people in bright robes made their way to the front of the church.

Narrator 1 The jester looked at his own bright clothes with sadness. Though they had made many people smile, they didn't seem appropriate for this splendid place, and in a tiny, sad voice he whispered to himself,

Jester They are all worthier than me.

Narrator 1 Then he heard a small noise from just inside the porch.

Narrator 2 Moving closer, he saw a young woman with a baby in her arms. It was dark now, and rain had started to fall. She huddled against the wet protecting her child, and spoke defensively,

Woman I just wanted to shelter from the rain. I'd better go.

Jester No, wait.

Narrator 2 He ran to a nearby shop and bought an umbrella, and brought it back to the woman and her child.

Jester For you. But why don't you go and sit in the church for a while? At least it's warm and dry.

Woman I don't know anyone, and I've no collection – and they won't want me!

Jester I can come and sit with you, and I've got a bit of money for the collection. Anyway they're your family in Christ. You need to meet each other!

Narrator 2 The woman smiled at the jester's smile, and together they went into the church. She was made welcome and, still smiling, he later went on his way.

Narrator 1 As the day drew to a close, the jester returned to his comfortable home and made something to eat. He was grateful for all he had, and felt secure in his faith.

But there was still a sense of regret within him, and pushing his meal to one side, he prayed:

Jester   Thank you, Lord, for the good things we have and which we share:
for friendship, for your Spirit,
for faith, hope and love . . .
but Lord, one day I pray that I will see you.
Today I might not be good enough, or clever enough,
but one day, Lord, one day . . .

Narrator 2   The Jester's voice faded away and the only noise in the room came from the flames crackling in the hearth. The quietness gradually filled his heart and his mind with peace. Then it seemed to him that a voice spoke directly to him.

Christ   Dear, dear friend. I came to you today, as you asked!

I was cold and miserable. You played with me and cheered me up.

I came.

I was despairing, and you lifted me up.

I came.

I was young and vulnerable and lost.
You brought me into my Father's house and made me safe.

I came in many ways.

You opened your heart to me, and you embraced me.

Narrator 1   The Jester frowned, then smiled, and shook his head so that the bells jangled with joy, his delight was so great.

Jester   You came . . . I never knew . . . I never knew . . .

Narrator 2   And he rested his head on his arm and fell asleep.

Talking heads

Away from the parish recently, I slipped into a church for their main Sunday Worship. I am always nervous going somewhere new and feel vulnerable. This time, the feeling increased as I first of all struggled with a huge, closed medieval door, which then closed after me with a great noise, and then took books from a sidesman (or was he the warden?) who gave me a pleasant smile, but said nothing. At the end of the service when everyone sat and chatted with their neighbour, except me, feelings of inadequacy overwhelmed me and I scurried out (there was no minister to say good-bye), struggling once again with the enormous door, which again slammed shut behind me. The next visit was the same, except the door didn't slam behind me.

It made me think critically about the welcome we give to people who come into our own church, for I suspect that we are warm and caring only when we notice new people. However, the newcomers, if they are anything like me, might have all types of thoughts going through their heads . . . and so can members of the congregation.

You could adapt this sketch to take in the grumbles you hear in your church.

This sketch needs four people in two pairs, A/B pair standing back-to-back and C/D pair facing each other. The voice of Jesus stands between them:

Voice A: newcomer
Voice B: sidesman
Jesus
Voices C and D: members of the congregation

A   I'm late, I'm flustered, shall I go in?

B   I've closed the door against the wind. All the usuals have arrived.

A   Will this door open? I need two hands. Is it the right entrance? It's awfully heavy.

B   Oh, a latecomer. I'd better get some books. I wonder who she is? She's a bit late.

A   Where do I sit? Everybody looks at home here, better not intrude. Here will be fine, out of the way.

C   Nice to see new faces in church.

D   Makes you wonder why they come, though.

C   Had a funeral this week, I think. Old Mrs Edmunds.

D   That might be her niece then. Shame she didn't come while the old lady was alive.

C   People don't these days. Unforgivable, really.

Jesus   Do not judge, and you will not be judged.
Do not condemn, and you will not be condemned.
Forgive, and you will be forgiven.
Luke 6:37

A   Daniel, will you stop pulling! We are going to church!

B   *(To him/herself, quietly)* Not another one with a noisy child. *(Smiling brightly)* Here is your service book . . . and service sheet . . . and there's *Mission Praise*. You'll find Bibles and hymn books in the pews.

A   I didn't know I'd get a library . . . Daniel! Stop it. Now I've dropped all the books.

B   Never mind. *(Huge sigh)* I'll pick them up.

C   Lots of children in church today.

D   Well, it is a family service.

C   Blimey, I forgot. You don't think they'll have us doing those action songs again?

D   Probably. Why do people bring young children? It's just not the place for them. Just look at that young woman struggling with her books! Oh, she's dropped them, poor soul.

C   She'll find it hard picking them up with the pews so narrow. Why do people bring little ones into church? It isn't the place for them.

Jesus Let the little children come to me;
Do not stop them . . . truly I tell you,
Whoever does not receive the kingdom of God as a little child
Will never enter it.
Mark 10:14-15

A Why do I bother? It's such a struggle getting all the kids to church. Still, at least it might help them get into a church school.

B I see she's here again – I wonder how long it will last?

A Oh look, there's Natasha coming in with the choir. I wish she'd smile a bit.

B Vicar shouldn't let the church be used like this. It's not right, coming just to get a reference for St Elphin's.

A I feel guilty doing this, but they say it's the best way. Show your face, get a good reference from the Vicar. And she needs to go to St Elphin's – it's the best school around.

(Pause)

I wish I understood what was going on in this service. I wish I knew about Jesus, about bread and wine – I feel so guilty!

B Look at her – hasn't a clue where she's up to in the service. And wants to get her child into St Elphin's School? Fat chance!

A I hope our Natasha appreciates this.

Jesus Why do you see the speck in your neighbour's eye,
But do not notice the log in your own?
. . . You hypocrite, first take the log out of your own eye
and then you will see clearly to take the speck out of your neighbour's eye.
Luke 6:41-42

C   Did you hear Madeleine going on at the PCC?* She wants more modern things sung during the services.

D   But people won't know them.

C   Just what I said. But she said, well, you can learn, just as you learned the old ones.

D   But you can't teach an old dog new tricks.

Jesus Of course you can teach an old dog new tricks, you just have to be patient. But then again, you have to consider whether they *need* to learn new tricks!

C   Madeleine said that we should have less Sunday school and more family services. She said newcomers would understand more.

D   She might be right. But then again, perhaps church is more than the service. Perhaps *we* can do more to help them understand and to welcome them.

Jesus The Spirit of the Lord is upon me, because he has anointed me to bring good news to the poor.
He has sent me to proclaim release to the captives
and recovery of sight to the blind; to let the oppressed go free,
to proclaim the year of the Lord's favour.
Luke 4:18-19

* *The PCC is the Parochial Church Council, a group of people, mostly elected, who help to run each parish church. You may have elders in your church or a leadership team.*

The Belladonica Tapes

'The Belladonica Tapes' was, of course, inspired by C. S. Lewis, who wrote
The Screwtape Letters. *This sketch was written for a service at the beginning*
of Lent when we wanted to introduce the Lenten themes. It formed the first
of a series for Lent called 'Friends of Jesus?' – sometimes the people and
concepts that appear to be 'Jesus friendly' are just the opposite. We need
to be able to perceive what is bad as much as we embrace what is good.

Narrator   Some of you may have heard of C. S. Lewis, the man who wrote *The Lion, the Witch and the Wardrobe*, and who published a little book of correspondence which passed between a senior devil, Screwtape and his nephew, Wormwood, an exceedingly junior devil.

These letters were written during the years of the Second World War and made fascinating reading. Since then, we have heard very little of these two servants of Lucifer, but modern technology is far too tempting for the likes of these demons to ignore, and so, with the help of modern bugging devices, we can tune into the conversations of another poisonous couple.

We bring you a transcript, not of the *Screwtape Letters* but of the Belladonica Tapes . . .

The phone rings and is picked up by Uncle Arsenicus, an Important Being in the Underworld which some call hell . . .

Arsenicus   My dear niece! What a joy, what a delight! Not having heard from you for positively decades, to what do I owe this present honour? For honour it must be if someone as lowly and inept as you can find it in you to ring and contact your old uncle . . .

Belladonica   Lowly is right, Uncle! I have recently been given the privilege of descending into the Chaos of the Underworld and am now, not your underling but your equal – and you are the first to hear my good news!

Arsenicus   *(The smile quite wiped off his face)* To hear you speak those awful words, 'Good News' reminds me why I did not recommend you for promotion! You sound just like the Enemy.

Belladonica   And it is him I have come to talk to you about – the one whose name we dare not mention – the Son who died. For you were there, were you not, when our Lord and Master, Lucifer, tried to befriend and entice him when he went into the desert to pray? You were one of the ones assisting, putting beautiful pictures into the Enemy's mind. Which, of course, he resisted . . .

Arsenicus   And why would you want to open old wounds? Our Lord Lucifer would not be pleased to hear you refer to that moment of utter calamity . . .

Belladonica   I mention it only because he himself has given me the task of tempting a church that is beginning to show disappointing signs, and as I can't go to our Lord Lucifer to ask why he failed . . . I thought I would come to you.

Arsenicus   *(Spluttering)* How dare you! How can you talk of failure when you see all that has been achieved in the last two thousand years? Or even the last hundred years?

Is it failure to have continuous warfare? Is it failure to see different races hacking each other to pieces, to know that one in three marriages will fall apart or that untold thousands will become our slaves through drug abuse?

No! All this is down to temptation and carefully planned seduction. Failure indeed! Haven't you seen my colleague Pratterling's masterly deception with statesmen, convincing them that greed and oppression is the only way to succeed, or the ways in which Lustering has undermined marriage?

Belladonica   *(Interrupting)* But the fact remains, *dear* Uncle, that you and our Lord Lucifer failed, failed because the Enemy still lives today, and through the ones he calls 'the Faithful' – the ones who pray and listen to him, and resist the wiles of run-down, worn-out old devils like you and your cronies – he gains ground daily.

Arsenicus   Enough of your lies!

Belladonica But they aren't lies, are they uncle? For the church I have the honour to restore to our Lord Lucifer, is one under your responsibility, one which has indeed been faithful to the Enemy for decades, but which in this present climate of change could be enticed to a broader path, welcoming all philosophies and beliefs and losing all faith along the way. An enthusiastic young tempter could have a field day befriending the friends of the Enemy . . .

Arsenicus And how do you know that is not what's happening? There have been some promising developments . . .

Belladonica *(Interrupts again, her voice rising with indignation)* Know? Know? I know because I was present at their prayer meeting. I know because I have seen their generosity. And most of all, I know because I listen to them considering ways in which new families cannot just be welcomed, but helped to get closer to the Enemy! Or how they can help those who are lost and lonely, how they can learn – yes, learn – from missionary agencies!

(She sneers) Oh yes, I know a great deal – and I also know the chinks in their armour – which you, once again have failed to see! *(She laughs a wicked triumphant laugh)* Once again, dear Uncle, you have failed –

Narrator With a great crackling and interference, the conversation was lost. We can only surmise what Arsenicus' response would be to the niece he hates so much! But perhaps if we, for just a moment, put ourselves into Belladonica's shoes (and if indeed, demons do wear shoes, hers would be extremely tall and red stiletto heels!), we might begin to see the chinks in our armour; we might identify the ways in which we step out of our Father's protection, and see ways in which malice, thoughtlessness and deliberate unkindness undermine the work of God, whereas actively seeking out his will protects and strengthens us.

Let's take a minute of silence to think about these things, and then confess them to God, who loves us and will forgive us and help us to start again.

A prayer of confession follows.

Moustapha, the first Christmas mouse

There is a legend, I am told, on the Island of Guernsey, that at midnight on Christmas Eve, all the animals kneel to worship the newborn King. St Paul's letter to the Romans also reminds us that 'creation waits with eager longing for the revealing of the children of God' (Romans 8:19).

It's only a short leap from there to imagine Christmas through the eyes of a mouse . . .

Narrator 1   This is the story of Moustapha, the forefather of all church mice. Moustapha was the mouse who saw Jesus. He very nearly didn't, but Moustapha was a very determined mouse, and this is his story.

Narrator 2   It was a day like many others for Moustapha bar Moysha. He, like his parents before him, was a temple mouse. It meant that he had to put up with some very long services, but on the other hand, he never went hungry. There was always plenty of parchment to nibble on, and because there were often markets in the temple courts, Moustapha was a well-fed mouse, and a mouse with a full tummy is a happy mouse.

Narrator 1   But not everyone liked mice. Some of the women screamed when they saw him, and this rubbed off on the animals who also lived in the courts of the temple and the nearby streets. Cats and dogs, horses and donkeys, pigs and goats, young calves and lambs, doves, sparrows and pigeons all lived in the temple courts. And, it has to be said, they looked down on little mice who scurried here and there, looking for titbits and rarely raising their heads to see the great world beyond.

Narrator 2   But some of the animals did see and hear of things happening beyond the temple courts, and one day, a pair of pigeons came swooping in, full of news and gossip.

They had seen many people gather together and set off to make a journey. There was a census taking place. They didn't know what a census was, but fortunately, the Wise Owl could tell them.

Owl   A census happens when the rulers decide that they want to know the names of all the people in the country, where they were born and where they now live.

Narrator 1   It seems that the Romans, who ruled Palestine wanted to know this very information, and the people had to travel to the place they were born in order to give the information needed. The pigeons saw people of all shapes, sizes and ages setting off for Bethlehem. There were men and women, children excited at the thought of going on a journey, and there was even a woman who looked very close to giving birth there with her husband. Eventually, they were all organised and the travellers left Jerusalem for Bethlehem. The older and wiser shook their heads, for it was winter and the weather was becoming very cold.

They watched this for a little while and then, as the people moved off on their journey, they continued with their day-to-day living, flying, eating and at night, sleeping.

Some time later the pigeons reported some more news to the animals in the temple courtyards.

Narrator 2   They had been flying over the king's palace when they saw three beautifully dressed men with lots of servants, camels and other animals go into the palace grounds. Being birds full of curiosity, and having the wings to take them higher than feet could tread, the pigeons followed the procession of rich men into the palace, and perched high on a ledge where they could see and hear everything, but few people could see them, and they listened very carefully.

It seemed that the rich men with their beautiful clothes were wise men, called Magi, who had been travelling for many months to see the newborn king.

Recently, a beautiful and unusual star had shone in the

sky, and had moved, guiding the Magi to Jerusalem and beyond. They wanted to know if King Herod had heard of this new little baby king.

Narrator 1   Herod shook his head – but he listened carefully to all the wise men had to say.

1st Wise Man   We have followed a star which has led us through many countries to Jerusalem, and we believe it will continue to guide us until we come to a place where there is a newborn king.

Narrator 1   King Herod questioned the wise men very carefully. If there was going to be another king in his land, he wanted to know exactly where this king was.

Herod   Where do you think this little king is – do you actually know?

2nd Wise Man   O yes, the new king will be in Bethlehem in Judea.

Narrator 2   Now the wise men were not to know this, but Herod was not a good man. He was a deceitful and cruel king who guarded his domain jealously, and the whisper of a new baby king threw him into a fit of rage – which he was careful not to show. The wise men didn't realise, but the pigeons did.

Smiling, Herod directed the wise men to Bethlehem, thinking that they could show him where this contender for his throne might be found.

Narrator 1   Now the pigeons were kind birds, even if they gossiped rather a lot, and they knew of King Herod's jealousy and temper. As the wise men prepared to leave, they flew out into the courtyard where they met Moustapha, the temple mouse, and told him all they had seen and heard.

Moustapha thought quickly. He was an inquisitive little mouse, but, like the pigeons, very kind, and he said to them:

Moustapha   Bethlehem is too far you to fly, but I can get there easily. Just watch!

Narrator 2	And with that, he scurried over to the nearest wise man's camel, ran up the camel's back and hid in its coat.
	80 miles later, and very shaken about, Moustapha all but fell off the camel's back. He shook his head, straightened his fur and looked all around him.
	He, and the wise men were in another courtyard, but one much smaller than the one in Jerusalem. It seemed to be by an inn and a stable. Moustapha asked a passing chicken what was happening. The chicken clucked with delight.
Chicken	You'll never believe it! We've had so many visitors, all the shepherds, and all the animals, we've even had a choir of angels up in the sky . . .
Moustapha	*(Interrupting)* Yes, yes, but why? Who were they coming to see?
Chicken	Why, the baby king of course! Look, I must go, my mummy's getting an egg ready for his mummy's breakfast.
Narrator 1	And with that, the chicken scuttled off into the stable.
Narrator 2	Moustapha thought the chicken must have gone into the wrong place in his excitement, and he started to go into the inn, but soon stopped when a very large and very stripy tabby cat uncurled herself and stood in his way.
Narrator 1	And hissed. Moustapha started to back away. Hissing cats needed to be taken very seriously but it seemed this cat was not as hostile as Moustapha thought.
Cat	And where do you think you are going?
Moustapha	*(Stammering dreadfully)* Oh, please don't eat me or chase me, Mrs Cat. I've only come for the baby king. I won't trouble you any more.
Narrator 2	And with that, he turned, ready to run away. But the cat had other ideas.
Cat	Well, you won't find him in the inn, nor will you find him in

the direction you're running. Turn around, young man and go into the stable. The dog will tell you where to go next.

Narrator 1 Moustapha couldn't believe his ears! His tail flew backwards and forwards and his whiskers twitched. Whenever had a cat not chased a mouse, and a dog had polite conversation with the same cat! This was very strange. He turned and walked cautiously into the stable. Well, what else was a mouse to do except follow the instructions of a cat who was kind?

Narrator 2 He entered the stable as quietly . . . as a mouse! But guarding the door was a dog. A dog not a lot larger than the cat, but a dog with lots of teeth. Moustapha didn't know what to say. The dog appeared to be smiling – and then he spoke!

Dog 'Ave you come to see our little king?

Narrator 1 It was all Moustapha could do to nod his 'Yes'.

Dog Then just go over to the manger, little friend, and you'll see our special child.

Narrator 2 Moustapha tiptoed over to the baby, and with cows and sheep and cats and other mice, he watched the baby yawn in his sleep and wriggle closer to his mother.

Narrator 1 For a moment he was stunned by what he saw, and what he knew in his heart to be the truth. Then, the moment changed as the wise men came in and gave the most wonderful gifts to the baby king.

The animals watched with delight as the humans, too, recognised the special-ness of this tiny child, but though they made soft sounds and sighs, the squeak of an agitated mouse could be heard above it all.

The cat, who had softly entered the stable to stand by the dog, frowned.

Cat Don't make such a noise, young man.

Moustapha   *(Squeaking more than ever)* I'm so sorry! I heard something dreadful and I don't know who to tell.

Narrator 2   The cat looked at him kindly, and waited while the distraught little mouse poured out all that the pigeons had told him, and their fears for the newborn king.

The cat looked at him even more kindly.

Cat   I don't think you need worry, just look up there.

Narrator 1   Moustapha raised his little head, and nearly fell over in amazement. For there, sitting in the rafters were angels – and he'd never seen angels before!

Cat   They'll look after our little king even more than we can.

Narrator 2   And it was true, for no sooner had the Magi gone back to their own countries than Joseph gathered up his little family and took them to Egypt.

Narrator 1   One of the angels warned him just in time that bad things were going to happen, and so Mary, Joseph and little Jesus had to run away to Egypt, for Herod sent his soldiers to do dreadful things. But the holy family was safe.

Narrator 2   And the little mouse?

Narrator 1   Well, he was safe too. Badly shaken by the sound of the soldiers' armour rattling, and their large horses stamping and snorting, he hid for a while in the fur of the cat, till he realised that he needed to get back to his home, to the temple courts, and so, being a brave little mouse, he clung onto the tail of a fine soldier's horse.

Narrator 2   Back at the temple courts he told the pigeons his wonderful story of a baby king and of angels and of cats and dogs who didn't fight or chase little mice. Some believed him and some didn't, but Moustapha didn't really care. He might be back in the world where cats chased mice and dogs chased cats, but he had seen Jesus. And he would never forget!

What is Communion?

This little sketch and the following prayers were the result of brainstorming with our teenage confirmation group. We had been talking about Communion, and wondered just what other people came to church thinking about, and this is very much their sketch.

The group also wanted to plan a service and to put their ideas into practice. They presented sketch A, with the help of some members of our congregation, at the beginning of a service which was to explore the meaning of the Eucharist. One of the confirmees acted as 'link' (Voice 1) and the others (Group) all chorused the response to the other voices, whom we hijacked as they came into church, adult and child! The Voices were scattered around the church and the confirmation group were gathered at the front shouting out their response.

Also included are other ideas we incorporated into the service to clarify the need for Confession (B) and to make our prayers a bit more visual (C).

NB If you decide to take up our ideas for confession, you will need to hand out small pieces of paper to your church members as they arrive and make sure there are pens and pencils available.

A At the start of the service

Voice 1   Some people think that Holy Communion is just bread and wine, but it's that and more.

They think that you have to be really good all the time – or at least seem to be good – but God is much more concerned with who we are and what our attitude is:

Voice 2   My dad's mean. He made me stop texting and start tidying!
Group   *That's not communion.*

Voice 3   I am so fed up with my children; they never tidy up, they always have something else to do . . .
Group   *That's not communion.*

Voice 4   That new girl in my school, she thinks she's better than me. I'll show her!
Group   *That's not communion.*

Voice 5 I'm glad I'm going to church. I wonder if Freda Baggins will have that dreadful hat on again!

Group *That's not communion.*

Voice 6 I hope I don't see Derek today; he's so boring!

Group *That's not communion.*

Voice 7 I hate church. I don't believe and don't see the point.

Group *That's not communion.*

Voice 1 So, if that's *not* communion, what is?

Voice 2 It's nice coming out with Mum and Dad, even if it is to church.

Group *That's communion.*

Voice 3 I feel so tired; it will be good to sit and listen, to sing and pray.

Group *That's communion.*

Voice 4 I feel sorry for that new girl, she doesn't quite fit in. I wonder if I can help.

Group *That's communion.*

Voice 5 I'm so glad I'm going to church. I'll see if Freda needs a lift, and we can sit together. Perhaps she'll help me going up to Communion; my knees are awfully stiff these days.

Group *That's communion.*

Voice 6 Derek's so lonely. I wonder if a few of us could go out together; perhaps we can sort something out . . .

Group *That's communion.*

Voice 7 I hate church, it's so boring. But if so many other people come, there could be something. Perhaps I'll listen, and if I try to pray, maybe someone will hear . . .

Group *That's communion.*

B Before the Confession

Voice 1   Why do we confess our sins?

One of the ministers or youth leaders explains that sin puts barriers up between us and our friends and families; that it causes problems and makes God seem very distant. However, he only seems distant. He is really very near and just waiting to destroy those barriers we have erected.

Go on to tell the congregation about Confession and Absolution: when we confess our sins God forgives is so completely that it is as if he has set fire to them and all that is left is ashes.

The Absolution then affirms that God does forgive, has forgiven us, and will give us all a new beginning.

Then, invite the congregation, who should have all been given small pieces of paper, to write a word or a phrase which summarised some sin they wish to confess. The confirmees collect them, put them into a metal bowl and we set them alight.

(We had not bargained for the coloured paper used smouldering instead of burning, and sending off a dreadful smoky smell, which had the choir coughing and one of the Readers scurrying to find water! Test the burning power of your paper beforehand!)

C Intercessions

One of the young people made a huge picture of the church using coloured paper for each different part. All of them had spent some time at the confirmees' meeting devising appropriate prayers and pictures to accompany them (mostly discovered on the computer's Clip Art, but some were simple line-drawings).

As the prayers were read out, the little pictures were stuck with Blu tack onto the large, coloured church.

Prayer for	Symbol
Church	bricks
the world	the earth
the local community	people
people in need	cross
ourselves and our church	bread and wine

PART TWO

Old Testament Sketches

After Goliath
1 Samuel 18:1-16

All the best novels stop at a good point. They leave us with a feel-good factor and with the good guys having won. Our memory of the story of David and Goliath tends to be like that. We all remember the slight boy coming out unarmed and slaying the large and very evil Goliath – but though our memory of David might stop there, his story continues and, like the curate's egg, it was only good in parts. David was generally one of the good guys, but even good guys have their weaknesses and don't always learn from their experiences.

This story is probably best told by one good narrator, with others taking the roles of David, Goliath, etc. and miming their responses.

Narrator   You have to admit, it was a pretty amazing feat to have pulled off: a young man, little more than a boy, taking on Goliath, and winning!

There had been a deadlock for days: Goliath and his army on one hill, and Saul and the Israelite army on another. Each morning Goliath, literally a giant of a man dressed in the most splendid armour, would come out and challenge any one of the Israelites to meet him, man to man. He said that if he won the fight, the Philistines would rule the Israelites, but if the Israelites won, they would have the upper hand!

On the face of it, it seemed like a good idea – especially if you were a Philistine! No great slaughter and with this seemingly invincible giant stealing the show, it appeared that they couldn't lose.

Naturally enough, the Israelites were reluctant to take up the challenge. All their fighting men were at least a foot shorter and four stone lighter, and even though their leader, King Saul, offered them great riches and power, none of them would be tempted . . . well would you?

So it went on, day after day. Goliath would appear and shout out his challenge and insult the Israelites. Then one day a young lad appeared, bringing food for his brothers. He heard the challenge being given yet again, and you all know the rest of the story – or the ending to this particular chapter at least!

David, still a teenager, went and faced Goliath, with no armour to protect him and only his sling and five small, smooth pebbles that he had picked up from the ground. Goliath mocked the boy and despised him, but all it took was one small stone and a perfect aim, and Goliath, the invincible giant, was dead.

As he promised, Saul made young David very rich. Gold and fine clothes came his way, he lived with Saul and his son, Jonathan, and he and Jonathan became as close as brothers.

It seemed that David couldn't put a foot wrong. Whatever Saul told him to do, whether it was a simple task or hard, David did it and was always successful.

They arrived home after many battles and adventures and the crowds came out on the streets to welcome them. Saul was delighted – till he heard what they were shouting:

Saul has slain thousands,
But David has slain tens of thousands.

His pride in David turned to great jealousy. Everyone loved the boy – the crowds, his army, even his own son Jonathan was besotted with David – and Saul's envy started to eat away at him. Round and round in his mind went the words:

(Saul)   *They're giving David all the credit for the battles we've won. But where does this leave me? He'll want my kingdom next!*

Saul's jealousy turned to an obsessive desire to get David out of the way, and he even tried to kill the young man, but David managed to escape.

Friendship had been destroyed by envy. And envy was to be Saul's downfall. He simply could not control his anger towards the young, handsome man who had initially been his saviour.

David eventually became the next king and under his leadership, Israel was faithful to God and the Ark of the Covenant was brought back to Jerusalem.

David seemed invincible and omnipotent. Unfortunately, he started to think he really was and this led to some foolish behaviour.

For instance, he had a wife – or even two – but he just happened to see a woman called Bathsheba and he thought she was the most beautiful woman he had ever seen. So beautiful in fact he just had to have her – to marry her.

Which might have seemed greedy, as he already had some wives; and as Bathsheba was also married to Uriah, a soldier in David's army, it was also not possible . . .

But, we aren't talking of just any old king here, we're talking of David, who, as an adolescent, brought the mighty Goliath tumbling down with a little creative thinking and some dexterity with a sling.

David weighed up this current problem in much the same way. He no longer needed a sling, but creative thinking could come in useful. Bathsheba was the goal – her husband Uriah was the enemy to be slain.

As he had eliminated Goliath from the picture, so David set about removing Uriah.

It was simple, really. As kings have the power to do, he spoke to Uriah's commander in the army, and consequently at the very next battle, guess who found himself in the firing line?

Uriah.

And, not unexpectedly, he was killed.

With all the obstacles removed, David was free to marry Bathsheba, the woman of his dreams. She wept for Uriah, but still married the king and they had a son.

And lived happily ever after?

Well, no. That really doesn't happen, except in novels, and this was real life.

God intervened through the prophet Nathan. David realised how arrogant he had become and how cruelly he had acted, and he repented. He tried to make amends, but nothing could bring Uriah back and David had to learn to live with his despicable behaviour and the consequences of his actions.

Talents, like power, can be used for good and for bad. David initially used his clever mind to slay Goliath, to help Saul and to discern the will of God. But with regard to Bathsheba, he used both talent and power for his own selfish desires.

Will you slay a Goliath – or will you spoil someone's life?

You have the same choices as David.

Jeremiah

Jeremiah 1:1-10

Sometimes Bible stories need very little help; they can be retold with just a little extra animation.

A little while ago, our Bishop licensed a Church Army captain, Andrew, as our Youth Co-ordinator and, as his priority was to be working with young people, we wanted them to participate in the service, which of necessity was a fairly formal one.

Andrew had chosen this reading from Jeremiah, chapter 1 and we simply expanded the narrative a little, and gave Jeremiah a voice. The two narrators stood one in the pulpit and one by the lectern, and a young Jeremiah came slowly up the aisle to kneel at the chancel steps.

Narrator 1   In the dim recesses of time, about six hundred years before the birth of Jesus, Judah was in a pretty bad state. The country had been conquered and the able-bodied men and women of Jerusalem taken to Babylon as slaves. And they were not happy.

Narrator 2   'By the waters of Babylon we sat down and wept,' they mourned. 'We hung up our harps and would not sing for those who had taken us as prisoners. How could we sing the Lord's song to those who mock us?'

Narrator 1   They hated the Babylonians with a vengeance.

Narrator 2   And they wallowed in their misery.

But the Lord was not impressed with such behaviour. He wanted his voice heard and action taken.

Narrator 1   And so he looked around for the right person to speak out to the captives –

Narrator 2   and as he cast his eyes around, they lighted on . . .

Narrator 1   Jeremiah!

Narrator 2   Jeremiah, not a little surprised at hearing his name echoing around him, paused, looking puzzled. And again, his name was spoken.

Narrator 1   Jeremiah!

Narrator 2   And he realised it was the voice of the Lord calling out to him, and he fell on his knees in fear and wonder.

Narrator 1   Jeremiah. I have known you before you were even conceived. Before you were born, I blessed you, and appointed you to be my spokesman to the nations –

Narrator 2   Jeremiah interrupted hastily, stammering in his concern to be heard,

Jeremiah   (With great feeling) Your spokesman, Lord? b-b-but I'm young – only a ch-child!

Narrator 2   But the Lord shook his head at Jeremiah and said,

Narrator 1   Only a child? Don't be foolish! Stand up Jeremiah. You're an adult and quite capable of carrying a simple message!

Jeremiah   B-b-but –

Narrator 1   Get up, Jeremiah, and forget such foolish things. Don't say 'I am only a child!' for I have a task for you. You must go to all to whom I send you, and say whatever I command you. You must confront them and not be afraid, for I am with you always.

Narrator 2   Jeremiah bowed his head in acceptance of the Lord's task,

Jeremiah   Let it be as the Lord says. I will try and do all that he wants of me.

Narrator 2   And the Lord blessed him and promised to give him the words to say and the ability to carry out the work that lay before him.

Narrator 1   And so it was that Jeremiah, the reluctant prophet, did all that the Lord had commanded him. It was often hard, and there were times when he feared for his life as he confronted the people of Jerusalem with the Word of God.

But he grew in faith, and his words are a legacy to us today of the great things God can do with those who listen to his voice and respond to his call.

Nehemiah
Nehemiah 1:1-11

We had been asked to host a service for Christian Unity one cold night in January. Members of the other churches in Wavertree were invited to come and our new Bishop of Warrington had agreed to preach. We wanted to emphasise the need to work together in order to grow together, and Nehemiah and his dedication to rebuilding the walls and the Temple of Jerusalem was our starting point. Nehemiah's story was retold by two narrators.

Narrator 1   Good evening. Our story tonight concerns a man called Nehemiah, whom most people have not heard of, and who lived about two and a half thousand years ago, but who was also a great hero.

Narrator 2   Not a hero like David was, killing Goliath, but a hero nevertheless.

Narrator 1   He was Jewish, but lived at the court of a Persian king as the king's cup-bearer – a very privileged position for one whose people had been defeated in war and taken from their home to serve as slaves in a foreign land.

Narrator 2   And Nehemiah was probably as content as he could be, given that he was a servant in a foreign land.

Narrator 1   Then one day his peace was shattered. His brother Hanani and some other Jews arrived with terrible news:

Narrator 2   They had been back to Jerusalem and were shocked at what they had seen.

Narrator 1   The great wall of the city had been so damaged by war that it was broken down in many places and fire had destroyed the gates.

Narrator 2   Nehemiah was devastated. Jerusalem was the spiritual home of his people. To think of it damaged by the ravages of war deeply distressed him, and he wept and mourned for the city he loved so much.

Narrator 1   He took immediate action –

Narrator 2   but not the action that you maybe would have expected.

Narrator 1   He fasted for three days, and as he fasted he prayed to God.

Narrator 2   His prayer initially was not for guidance,

Narrator 1   it was one of confession, of repentance for all the wrongs his people had ever done:

Narrator 2   'O great and terrible God, who faithfully keeps his promise to all who love you and obey your commandments, hear my prayer, which I make for me and my fellow Israelites.

'I confess the sins which we have committed against you . . . we have broken your laws and been unfaithful . . .'

Narrator 1   Only then did Nehemiah turn to asking God for help.

Narrator 2   For the Lord had said to his people, 'If you are unfaithful you will be taken from your homeland and scattered among all the other nations, but if you return to me – if you acknowledge your sinful ways and ask forgiveness – then I will bring you back to Jerusalem.'

Narrator 1   And he ended by asking God to let him be successful in his task.

Narrator 2   For Nehemiah had a plan.

Narrator 1   He went to the king shortly after making this prayer, and as he handed him the cup of wine, the king noticed that Nehemiah was looking unhappy, and asked why.

Narrator 2   Nehemiah told him about the state of Jerusalem. He asked permission to go back there to build and restore it to its former glory, and told the king how he had prayed about this very matter.

Narrator 1   The king not only agreed, but gave him as much help as he needed to make the long journey in safety.

Narrator 2   The work was hard and sometimes dispiriting, but Nehemiah succeeded in his task. The walls of Jerusalem were rebuilt, new gates were constructed, and the Temple was also restored. People worked together, made plans together and prayed together.

Narrator 1   Sometimes there were disagreements and, even worse, there were plots concocted against Nehemiah, and yet they succeeded in a task that seemed impossible.

Narrator 2   The Jews were a tiny group of people in a vast Gentile empire and many of them were slaves. They may well have felt demoralised and hopeless. Those left behind in Jerusalem would have been too young, too old or too weak to have been taken as slaves. The restoration of Jerusalem looked impossible.

Narrator 1   But one man had faith and courage.

Narrator 2   Faith led Nehemiah to pray, and courage led him to ask the king of Persia for help.

Narrator 1   What could we achieve if we prayed together . . .

The alternative Genesis
Genesis 1:1-4

Creation is a hot issue in these 'green' days and humanity's onslaught on the earth and its resources is a topic which can be addressed at Harvest and also at Rogation. We are a church in the heart of the city, but every couple of years, we hold a 'Rogation for the City' service. We walk out into the churchyard and walk to the four corners, praying for different aspects of city life and beyond. We have used this sketch to start the service as a reminder that it isn't God who gets things wrong!

Narrator   When God created the earth and all that is in it, he left making men and women until the very end. Have you ever wondered why? Then just listen to all that might have taken place had man been created first of all . . .

   In the beginning, when God created the universe, the earth had no shape, nor any light. It was empty, and it was a very lonely place to be. So God, who was about to create a wonderful world, first of all created a human being, and gave him a name – Adam.

Adam   That's me! I'm Adam. I'm the first thing God has made. So, I must be pretty important.

Narrator   God ignored this. He had far too much on his mind; after all, he had a whole entire world to create, and though Adam was reasonably important, there were other things to be considered.

God   It is so dark here, you just can't see a thing. Something has to be done!

Narrator   And so God spoke in a very loud voice:

God   Let there be LIGHT!

Narrator   And it was just as though a million light bulbs had been turned on, the light was so dazzling.

God realised that good though it was, no one could live with such bright light all the time, so he separated light from darkness, and was well pleased.

God   Look Adam, don't you think this is wonderful? A moment ago, there was only darkness all around, and now we have light as well. I think we'll call them Night and Day.

Adam   Well I suppose that's all pretty clever; but are you sure you've done the right thing making it light sometimes and dark the rest of the time? After all, when it's dark, we can't see a thing, and though it doesn't matter too much now, when you have made more things, when it's dark we'll just keep bumping into them all the time. If I were you, I'd make it light all the time. Let's have daylight all day! And while you are at it, my feet are getting very wet. I think you should do something about that as well!

God   But little man, you don't know the rest of my plans. You are so new, you don't realise that you will need to sleep, and who wants to sleep when it's light and there are lots of things to do? And what about the plants and animals and birds? They will need time to rest as well –

Adam   *(Interrupting)* Plants? Animals? Birds? What are they? And what's 'sleep'? Could you just concentrate for a moment – my feet are getting wetter by the minute. *(Continues to grumble through the next bit of narrative)*

Narrator   And God heaved a huge sigh *(God sighs loudly)* and began to wonder if he had done the right thing in making man first. Perhaps Eve would have been a better helper. It was not a bad idea. But then Adam's grumbles once again disturbed God's musings.

God   All right, little man. Let's dry your feet. *(Loudly)* Let there be a dome to divide the water and to keep it in two separate places.

Narrator   And Adam looked down and saw water rushing away from his feet and dry land appearing. Then he looked up and saw beautiful blue above him. God looked at him and said proudly,

God   There you are little man, you are now standing on dry ground. The water I shall call sea and the beautiful blue I shall call sky and –

Narrator   But Adam, dusting the mud off his feet, interrupted again:

Adam   It's all right you talking about what you've just done, but that blue – what did you call it? Sky. Well it's a bit boring, isn't it? I mean, it's . . . just blue. Can't you create a few more colours to put in it? And while you're at it, what about this dry ground we're stood on – there's nothing else, just dry ground. It's all a bit empty, don't you think?

Narrator   God looked rather cross, but replied patiently:

God   One thing at a time, little man, there's still the rest of eternity to make things in . . .

Narrator   And he started making the most wonderful creatures you could ever imagine, and you might, because you have seen some of them, but Adam hadn't, and he kept talking to God:

Adam   Why has the giraffe got such a long neck? Won't it get stiff? And why is that hippo so fat? And the elephant so big? And why am I so small? And why do you keep calling me 'little man'? And can't you make me bigger and more important? And don't you think buttercups should be pink and bluetits be green and –

Narrator   *(Interrupting)* God had heard enough.

God   ENOUGH!

Narrator   he roared, and in the silence that followed, he thought carefully about his next course of action.

            (Pause) Then he smiled, and said in a loud voice:

God   Let it be the beginning again.

Narrator   And it was. There were no animals, or birds or plants. There was no sky, or sea, no light or dark. And there was no Adam. And God saw that it was very good . . . and started all over again!

The voice of God

A joke did the rounds of our part of Liverpool a little while ago. A man was desperate to win the Lottery, and so he prayed to God. And he didn't win. A second time he prayed, and a third time, and still there was no jackpot win. He shouted at God, doubting his existence: 'I pleaded with you for help and you refused.' Suddenly a voice broke through his angry words: 'Meet me halfway. At least go out and buy a ticket . . .'

This wry comment on the way in which God communicates and supports us triggered this sketch.

Narrator 1   'In those days the voice of the Lord was rare; there were not many visions' (1 Samuel 3:1). *(Pause)*

Narrator 2   A man was preparing to take a small rowing boat out for the day, and he had hired one from a sailor at a well-known coastal resort.

Man   I want to hear the voice of God.

Sailor   *(Amusement in his voice)* Not much chance of that.

Narrator 1   He had taken the man's money and instructed him in the ways of safety when out at sea.

Sailor   You'll be too busy tending the boat.

Man   Oh, I don't know, out there with the wind and the waves, and perfect silence . . . Jesus used to go in a boat when he wanted to connect with the Father in heaven.

Narrator 2   The owner of the boat looked on the would-be sailor with laughter in his eyes and some concern.

Sailor   Just be careful. Let me check: you've got your life jacket, extra fuel for the engine, ropes and something warm to drink? You have all of those? And what about the radio?

Man   I have it – but I won't need it!

Narrator 1   The owner shook his head as the little boat sailed out to sea, and he made a mental note to be extra vigilant when the would-be sailor was due to return home.

Meanwhile, the man set out to sea, full of confidence that he could handle the little boat, and equally full of confidence that he would hear the voice of God. First of all, he rearranged some of the equipment in the little boat. He moved the container of fuel onto the seat at the other side of the boat so that he had more leg room, and he brought his flask and ice box of food closer. Of course, he mused, he might not touch the food. He might fast instead, but he would need the coffee for warmth.

Narrator 2   Yes, he would fast and God would speak to him and keep him safe. As he contemplated first the blue skies and the millpond sea, he spoke to God, but heard no response.

As clouds started to scud across the blue horizon, and little white horses danced on the waves, he tried to revel in the glory of God's creation, and he told God so. But God did not reply. His little boat took him further out to sea as the clouds turned dark and hostile, and the waves no longer danced but vented their fury on the little boat.

Narrator 1   But he wasn't used to the sea, and turning awkwardly to reach his flask of hot coffee, he stumbled and fell awkwardly onto the can of fuel which he had placed high on the seat instead of in the bottom of the boat. He knocked it over and out of the boat. It sank without trace, but the man had no qualms: God would protect him. He continued to sail out to sea.

Narrator 2   Still the man sailed further away from the coast. By now, the rain had started to fall, and the waves lashed the little boat. The man was swept overboard, but was saved from drowning by his life jacket and the rope provided by the owner.

Narrator 1   Finally, in desperation, he used his radio to call for help. He heard no response and presumed that, like God, they were not listening to him. He curled up in the bottom of the boat and prepared to die. Cynically, he recalled that only that morning, that blue and golden morning so full of promise, he would have used the phrase, 'prepared to meet his maker', rather than 'prepared to die'.

Narrator 2 The lifeboat found him some hours later, cold, wet and barely conscious, suffering from hypothermia, but still alive. The little boat had miraculously protected him, and the coastguards had received his call, but weather conditions had prevented their response being heard. They took the man to the safety of the shore and to a hospital. The man was delirious and as the doctors and nurses warmed his body and tended his wounds he kept calling out: 'He was silent. He wouldn't talk to me.'

Narrator 1 Finally, the man was moved from A and E to a ward for the night, just in case there was serious damage.

Warmed, and rested, the man finally fell into a deep sleep and woke to find a nurse sitting with him.

Nurse You're a lucky man. If the owner of the boat hadn't kept an eye out for you and alerted the coastguards, your story might have ended differently. Someone was looking after you.

Narrator 2 He looked at her with weary eyes.

Man I doubt it. No one cares about me. Not even God.

Narrator 1 The nurse appeared to ignore him.

Nurse You're not that experienced at sailing are you? Didn't they warn you about the sudden changes of weather on this bit of coast?

Man Yes of course, but I was desperate to get away and simply be with God. And he deserted me.

Nurse Didn't you worry when the extra fuel went overboard?

Man I didn't really think about it. I was desperate for peace and quiet, and to . . . connect. It was a matter of faith. A make-or-break time when, if I didn't hear God, I'd know he didn't exist. And it seems that he doesn't.

Nurse   Didn't you see the clouds gathering and think about coming home?

Man   I thought God would protect me, but why should he protect me when he couldn't even be bothered to talk to me?

Narrator 2   The nurse hardly seemed to hear this. She continued . . .

Nurse   The owner was concerned about you from the start. He checked the fuel can was filled and that you had a hot drink, he warned you about the changeable weather and he checked your radio was working. Before you signalled you were in trouble, he had alerted the lifeboat. They were already on their way.

Man   They heard my signal?

Nurse   Of course. You hired the boat from my husband. He only ever uses the best equipment. The boat is well cared for and the radio was state-of-the-art. Your signal was received. When you fell you must have damaged the microphone, but you were certainly heard.

Narrator 1   The man gave a small smile.

Man   Then thank your husband and the coastguards for their efforts. At least someone listened and responded.

Narrator 2   The nurse nodded and left him without another word.

Narrator 1   Later that day she went to church and prayed for him. She prayed for him and gave thanks for people like her husband and the men who manned the lifeboat, who cared and risked their lives for people like that sad, selfish man.

Narrator 2   She gave thanks to the God who spoke to her in so many ways, through the life she led and the people she met. She looked back on her day, to the people she had encountered, the wisdom she had received and the care she had given, the joy she had found in the blue skies and calm sea, and the concern she had felt when the sky darkened and the wind came up.

Narrator 1 She gave thanks for the different technologies and skills which saved lives in hospitals and at sea. And she wondered what God would have in store for her the next day . . .

Narrator 2 And the man lay warm and secure in his hospital bed, desolate and lonely, for he believed the voice of God was rare, and there were not many visions.

PART THREE

New Testament Sketches

Earache

Churches can be a source of great good, but they can also be the cause of endless frustration when different groups and individuals want different things! 'Earache' is the story of a body that didn't pull together and is introduced by St Paul's well-known description of the church as a body in 1 Corinthians 12.

This is not so much a sketch as 10 minutes of joyful confession involving one or two well-rehearsed, confident readers who can cope with chaos, children holding up pictures of an ear, a mouth, an eye, a foot, etc., and a congregation willing to listen hard and have some fun.

Have a short practice before the Introduction is read. Invite children to come and hold the pictures – we mounted them on long sticks so even little ones could take part and hold them high enough to see. Explain the principle – once they hear a body part being mentioned in the story, they have to shout out an appropriate response. The children will help by holding up a relevant picture. Then practice:

Shout out 'Ear!'

What should happen is the child holding the picture of an ear holds it up and the congregation shout back, 'Ere, 'ere! Then go through the rest of the body parts. When most people have the hang of it, let them sit back and take in St Paul's words to the Corinthians – then they can put it all into practice!

A An introduction to 'Earache' (the sketch)

A reading from St Paul's first letter to the Corinthians (1 Corinthians 12).

Paul was writing in the first century in response to a letter from the church in the city of Corinth. It seems as if there was squabbling in the congregation, some may have felt others weren't pulling their weight, while another group would complain that there was nothing left for them to do.

This is what Paul wrote to help them sort out their problems:

The body is a unity, though it is made up of many parts, and so it is with Christ: we are all part of him.

Now the body is not made up of one part but many. If the foot should say, because I am not a hand, I do not belong to the body, it would not for that reason cease to be a part of the body. And if the ear should say, because I am not an eye, I do not belong to the body, it would not for that reason cease to be a part of the body. If the whole body were an eye, where would the sense of hearing be?

But God has arranged the parts in the body, every one of them just as he wants them, and all are needed.

If one part suffers every part suffers with it. If one part is honoured, every part rejoices with it.

Now you are the body of Christ and each one of you is a part of it.

Just imagine what it would be like if the parts of your body didn't always work together . . .

B The Sketch

Narrator There was squabbling in the body – the ear

('ere, 'ere)

was not happy with the mouth.

(rabbit, rabbit)

'How can I possibly know what's going on if you don't talk to me?' the ear

('ere, 'ere)

grumbled. 'I can only hear. I can't see, I can only listen.'

But the mouth

(rabbit, rabbit)

pursed her lips very tightly and refused to utter a single word.

The problem for her was that the eyes

(ay, ay)

had seen a friend in the distance and had told the ears

('ere, 'ere)

The ears

('ere, 'ere)

wanted very much to hear what their friend had to say, for he was very funny, but the feet weren't quite fast enough to run and catch him and the mouth

(rabbit, rabbit)

refused to shout . . .

. . . because she said, 'I can't get a word in edgeways with him.'

'But', said the ear

('ere, 'ere)

– and lived to regret it – 'you get more than most in the rest of the time.'

Unfortunately, the eye

(ay, ay)

crinkled up at the corners, and the mouth

(rabbit, rabbit)

knew that he was quietly laughing at her, and so she clamped her lips firmly together and refused to say another word.

The other parts of the body were all totally disgruntled.

The feet

(stamp, stamp)

had tried hard to reach the friend, but didn't quite have the speed.

The hands

(clap, clap)

waved, but to a moving back they could not be seen.

Ear

('ere, 'ere)

could only hear, so only mouth

(rabbit, rabbit)

could have caught the friend's attention, and she chose to be awkward.

It took the brain to sort them all out, pointing out that just one part not pulling her weight caused the whole body to be ineffective – and to miss meeting a friend.

So the ear

('ere, 'ere)

told the mouth

(rabbit, rabbit)

that he understood her need to talk, and the mouth

(rabbit, rabbit)

that he understood her need to talk, and the mouth

(rabbit, rabbit)

apologised to the ears

('ere, 'ere)

and the eyes

(ay, ay)

and the hands

(clap, clap)

and the feet

(stamp, stamp)

for not co-operating, and on behalf of them all.

And the brain said to the heart, perhaps now we can get on with living!

When just one person doesn't pull their weight, the rest of the body/church/organisation suffers.

Eat your hearts out!

Luke 14: 15-24

Jesus told a story of a great feast where people were invited, but gave excuses not to come.

Here the scene is set for the Chef all chefs admire to throw the greatest party ever . . . but do they come? . . . They do not. However, though they didn't get to eat at the table of the greatest chef in the world, they certainly come by their just deserts!

Again, the story is told by two narrators with the main characters having short lines to say.

Voice 1   Even the Jamie Olivers of the world need to start somewhere, and that somewhere, for the most discerning, was with Edward Lovejoy.

Voice 2   He was the Chef of chefs, though by today's standards, relatively unknown, for he hated publicity and shunned the limelight.

Voice 1   Most people had heard his name, but couldn't quite place where.

Voice 2   TV? Radio? Newspapers? They weren't quite sure.

Voice 1   And they didn't really care.

Voice 2   But the people who knew always said he was the best. And they respected him enormously.

Voice 1   'An amazing talent,' said one top TV chef. 'We can only sit at his feet and listen,' said another. 'I'd peel the veg in his kitchen if he asked,' said a famous food columnist. Accolades were showered on him by all the famous foodies . . .

Voice 2   and when invitations for a huge party at a fantastic venue – Lovejoy's jealously guarded home – came through the letter boxes of chefs who had made a name for themselves on television, and in restaurants patronised by the rich and famous, they replied quickly.

Voice 1	Now Edward was determined to do the very best for his guests, and not only did he spend weeks gathering together food and the finest wines from the four corners of the earth, he also trained the finest team to prepare the food for his guests. No expense was to be spared, and no corners cut. He even thought about the safety of his guests, wining and dining as they would be, and provided chauffeur-driven cars for his friends.
Voice 2	The day dawned, and there was frantic activity in Lovejoy's kitchen and beyond as a marquee was raised in the gardens for entertainment after the banquet.
Voice 1	Inside, tables were laid with the finest linen, exquisite flowers and cutlery hand-crafted by the most experienced silver-smiths. Chandeliers shone on the diamond-cut glasses and finally, Lovejoy pronounced himself satisfied with the dining room and hurried back to the kitchen.
Voice 2	Round about lunchtime, his secretary came to him. She had received a couple of apologies – a wife wasn't well and a baby was due. A shadow crossed Lovejoy's face, but he shrugged it off –
Lovejoy	Understandable, I suppose –
Voice 2	and carried on supervising the cooking.
Secretary	And chef Van Hooten wanted to know which TV stations had been informed. I told him none – this was to be just for the chefs.
Voice 1	And Lovejoy nodded approvingly.
	Later in the afternoon, his secretary came back to see him. She looked worried.
Secretary	More people have sent their apologies, but they seem awfully thin. One has a headache, another is waiting for a lawn-mower to be delivered, and a third has his mother-in-law coming to stay. Do you want to hear the rest?
Voice 2	Lovejoy frowned.
Lovejoy	How many have you got there?

Secretary   Nearly half aren't coming – but the phone is still ringing.

Voice 2   By 5.30pm he'd had enough, and a comment from one of his guests told its own story.

Guest   If you'd had the TV crews here, we'd all have come!

Voice 1   Lovejoy was incensed. He called his staff together – those who weren't still cooking.

Lovejoy   Get on the phones now! Contact all those people we normally avoid: the tabloid reporters and paparazzi, the TV film crews and the gossip magazines – *Hello*, *Vanity Fair*, *OK* – all of them. Tell them to be here for 8.30pm for the meal of a lifetime.

Voice 1   Half an hour later he asked for an update.

Lovejoy   How are we doing – who's coming now?

Voice 2   All of them said yes, after all, they had never been allowed near his home, and they asked, can we bring a camera, extra reporter or video camera along?

Lovejoy   Yes, yes, of course they can. Whatever makes them happy.

Voice 1   And so from 8pm onwards Lovejoy's home was ablaze, not just with lights from chandeliers and fairy lights in the trees, but from the floodlights provided by a dozen television camera crews and countless flashing cameras.

Voice 2   And all those who had stayed at home saw the amazing spectacle reported on the 10 o'clock news – that reclusive, camera-shy Edward Lovejoy, the Chefs' chef, had opened his home to all those despised by the rich and famous, and provided exquisite food, suburb wines and fantastic entertainment for their enjoyment.

Voice 1   And whilst those newly invited guests consumed the best that the best chef in the world could offer in a blaze of publicity and camera light . . .

Voice 2   the ones who had declined stayed at home and ate their hearts out as Trevor McDonald told them exactly what they were missing!

The day the drinks ran out
John 2: 1-11

Everyone loves a good party! Good food, plenty to drink, witty conversation: a party lifts the spirits and generates goodwill, but sometimes the unexpected happens and a party needs to be rescued.

This is what happened in Cana of Galilee, when Jesus was at a party and the wine ceased to flow. It could have been a major catastrophe, but he saved the day and used the occasion to hint at things to come.

We updated the setting to Liverpool and included the names of local and church celebrities to make people laugh and, at its debut, the sketch provided a good introduction for a short sermon.

*You will want to use the names of people popular in your part of the world and perhaps a venue they will recognise.

Narrator 1   Good morning. Here we are again in church; all the decorations have been taken down, the Christmas tree has gone, and all seems rather flat and boring.

Narrator 2   So, we thought we would tell you a story. Once upon a time and long, long ago, a rich and important man threw a party –

Narrator 1   Hang on a minute. You just said, 'A long time ago' – parties still happen today you know.

Narrator 2   OK. Once upon a time, not so long ago –

Narrator 1   Probably as recently as this New Year's Eve –

Narrator 2   *(Continues as if there had been no interruption)* a rich and important man threw a party –

Narrator 1   Why do once-upon-a-time stories always assume that the rich and important are men?

Narrator 2   *(Sighs and tries again)* Once upon a time, a rich and influential woman threw a party for her *(pauses and throws a meaningful look at Narrator 1 and continues)* dearly loved son – it's not only the girls who get parties thrown for them—

Narrator 1 and it started off really well. Her house in Sinclair Drive* looked fabulous, with fairy lights along the drive and music setting a relaxed atmosphere; the food was good; the drink was even better, until . . .

Narrator 2 horror of horrors, the drink ran out!

Narrator 1 That's right! No champagne.

Narrator 2 No wine.

Narrator 1 No beer.

Narrator 2 Not even any fruit juice!

Narrator 1 This was a terrible, terrible thing to happen.

Narrator 2 So many important people were there.

Narrator 1 The Mayor and Roger Phillips* from Radio Merseyside.*

Narrator 2 Even Councillor Barbara Mace* had been invited.

Narrator 1 Not to mention Gill Jenkins.*

Narrator 2 The very best of Liverpool* society were partying away –

Narrator 1 eating, dancing, talking –

Narrator 2 but not drinking. And they were getting very thirsty.

Narrator 1 Very, very thirsty. But there was nothing to be had.

Narrator 2 And at that time of night, all the off-licences were closed.

Narrator 1 The situation was desperate indeed. No wine, or champagne. What could be done?

Narrator 2 The hostess – no longer with the mostest – turned to her close friend:

Narrator 1 'What can I do?' The offices are closed, and I can't turn water into wine,' she said, with despair in her voice.

Narrator 2   'No,' her friend said, thoughtfully. 'You can't. But I know who can.' And she turned away and disappeared into the crowd of thirsty party people.

Narrator 1   The hostess looked bewildered. 'What on earth are you talking about?' She hadn't a clue what her friend meant, and began to wonder if that was where all the wine had vanished to!

Narrator 2   Meanwhile, the friend was in a corner talking earnestly to her son. He was shaking his head. She was coercing him – as only mothers can do.

(Jesus and Mary mime a conversation where he is saying no, and she continues to plead)

Narrator 1   And finally a miracle occurs. He says yes.

Narrator 2   His mother knows him well enough to strike while the iron is hot. She finds some of the caterers and tells them to find buckets, bowls and baby baths, and to fill them with water.

Narrator 1   They look at her as if she is crazy.

Narrator 2   'She'll be telling us next to find a bath and fill it!' one says to the other.

Narrator 1   The friend smiles as she overhears the words. 'What an excellent idea!' she beams. 'Go and do it right now.'

Narrator 2   The caterers knew that party throwers had to be humoured, however irrational, and they went to do her bidding.

Narrator 1   No sooner had they filled every container in the house, than she told them to take jugs and fill them from the bath, the bowls and the buckets, and take them to the hostess to taste.

Narrator 2   She could not believe it. From the baby bath came fruit juice, from the bath came red wine, from the bowls came white wine, and from the buckets came the finest champagne. She was staggered, her guests were delighted, and her friend quietly pleased.

Narrator 1   Her son had saved the day.

Narrator 2   But the hostess was still puzzled. Who was this young man – and what had he just done? She had known him all her life, and now he had done this – was it a miracle? Could he have changed so much?

Narrator 1   She never forgot that evening, when water was changed into wine, and someone familiar was not really what he seemed at all.

The story of the wedding guests

Matthew 25:1-13

This was written for the Girl Guides when they were participating in one of our family services and we needed a sketch for girls!

The story of the young ladies who waited was also perfect, however, for a service that took place around the beginning of Advent.

As the narrators told the story, 10 Guides in two groups of five mimed the story. Instead of oil lamps, they had torches which they turned on and off at relevant moments.

*Dr Bruce is a much-loved member of Holy Trinity who is never, ever late. Ever. You may have someone like him in your church whose name will add a touch of laughter.

Narrator 1   Jesus told a story about 10 young women who were getting ready for a wedding recption.

Narrator 2   But this reception was very different to ones we have today.

Narrator 1   In the time of Jesus, great feasts were held to celebrate marriage, and the guests would go outside the bride's home and wait for the groom to come and claim her.

Narrator 2   Her friends would be waiting there to be the first to welcome him.

Narrator 1   And so, in our story, 10 girls went outside and prepared to wait.

Narrator 2   Night had fallen, and they had little oil lamps with them.

Narrator 1   Now, five of the friends were clever. They knew that men being men –

Narrator 2   especially bridegrooms –

Narrator 1   could not be relied on to arrive on time,

Narrator 2   and so they not only filled their little lamps with oil,

Narrator 1   they also took an extra supply.

Narrator 2   Wise girls!

Narrator 1   For men being men –

Narrator 2   except *Dr Bruce who always arrives early –

Narrator 1   they came late

Narrator 2   and the other girlfriends – who had taken just a little bit longer to do their hair, and paint their nails, and change their dresses at least twice – they had forgotton to bring extra oil and soon found themselves in the dark as their little oil lamps
     faltered
        spluttered
           and went out altogether.

Narrator 1   They begged their sensible friends to share their extra supplies of oil.

Narrator 2   But of course, if the girls had done this none of them would have light to see the bridegroom arrive – because he was very late indeed – and because they were sensible, they shook their heads.

Narrator 1   And the girls who were not so wise had to run to the shops to buy some extra oil.

Narrator 2   Because it was dark, they stumbled and fell. One broke the heel of her shoe and limped back;

Narrator 1   another snagged her hair on a low branch and they all heard the tearing of fabric as a dress was ripped by an unfriendly rose bush.

Narrator 2   Weary and dishevelled, they made their way back to the bride's house, their newly replenished lamps showing too clearly the ravages of their short journey.

Narrator 1   And though they had tried to be quick, they missed the excitement of the bridegroom arriving to claim his bride and the party had started when they arrived back.

Narrator 2   To crown it all, the bouncers on the door thought they were gate-crashers and wouldn't let them in!

Narrator 1   So you see it pays to think ahead, because you never know what will happen!

The wise and foolish builders

Matthew 7:24-27

I first saw the potential for this story when I lived close to Southport on the Lancashire coast, and all the houses close to the beach were built on sand. Subsidence was a real problem, especially when they were built not only on sandy soil but on sandy soil with a brook running by!

If you can get some hard hats for Fred and Joe to wear, so much the better.

*Change the names of the people and places to make it relevant to your community.

Narrator   Jesus said, 'Everyone who listens to me, and does what I say is like a man who chooses to build his house on good, firm foundations.'

Meet Fred and Joe. They will tell you all about the houses they want to build.

(Fred and Joe bow with a flourish to the congregation)

Fred   Building a house is a serious matter: it's expensive –

Joe   you're not kidding! –

Fred   it takes lots of time –

Joe   weeks and weeks and weeks –

Fred   Months and months and months, you mean! – and an amazing amount of hard work.

Joe   *(Nodding)* Where are you going to build your house, Fred?

Fred   *(Pulling his braces and looking smug)* I've found an excellent site in *Wavertree. The ground is good and hard, so it will take some digging to lay the foundations, but it will outlive me! Where are you building yours, Joe?

Joe   Oh, I've found a really good site down by the river: nice soft earth and easy to dig and lay foundations – should be simple, and a lot faster to build as well.

Fred   But you can't do that! You'll be building on sand – your house will fall over!

Joe   Not for ages, and it will go up faster and cost a lot less than yours. While you're still building, I'll be warm and snug inside.

Narrator   And he was too – that is until the rain fell so long and hard that the river flooded and the water seeped into Joe's house, damaging the foundations as well as his carpets and furniture and beautiful decorations.

Poor Joe!

As for Fred, when the rains came and the river flooded, he hadn't quite completed his house. The walls were finished, the windows put in and the roof on, but there was no furniture put in place. Fred had to wait while it was made, paid for and then delivered, so the house in *Wavertree felt bleak and cold despite the sturdy walls and well-fitting windows, and there were days that Fred felt quite depressed.

However, the day came when a furniture van rolled up outside his house full of chairs and tables, beds and all types of things.

It was delivered on the day that Joe's flood-damaged chairs were taken to the tip.

Clever Fred!

Whose house would *you* like to live in?

The woman in the bar

John 4: 1-42

Sometimes a change of scene can make a biblical story startlingly contemporary. The conversation Jesus had in Samaria with the woman by the well is one of these. Even in context, the story has much to tell us, but bring it into the third millennium and set it, not in the midday sun of Samaria, but the smoky, evening atmosphere of a Liverpool Docklands bar* and the subtleties somehow seem much more relevant.

Here we see Jesus relaxed and exchanging banter. We can imagine an attractive woman using her talent of flirtation, and an attractive man responding so that he can start sharing the good news with her.

Curiously, we don't know how the woman's story ends, for she fades away into the background but through her, others come to encounter Jesus.

* The setting, of course can be adapted to a situation closer to your own home town.

Narrator Ellie had not long come into the River Bar* to start her evening shift. It promised to be an interesting evening, with the match that afternoon at Anfield* being drawn between her home team, Liverpool,* and their rivals, Manchester United,* They didn't usually see any violence in this upmarket bar, but tongues alone could create an atmosphere.

She smoothed her hair, checked her lipstick and as she looked across the tables, one man caught her eye.

Usually, Ellie would have smiled back and indicated that orders were taken at the bar, but it was early and they were quiet and so she went over to him.

Man I want a drink.

Narrator She stared at him. Even by northern standards, the request was bald – no please, no thank you, just –

Man I'm thirsty. Get me a drink.

Narrator Ellie was taken aback.

Ellie	Most people come to the bar, and they ask nicely . . .
Narrator	She stopped abruptly, for as he looked up at her, she saw he was wearing a Man. United* shirt.
Ellie	This isn't the best place for someone like you.
Man	*(Smiling slightly)* I was thirsty, I needed a drink.
Narrator	The bar had started to fill up, and Ellie looked around nervously. It wouldn't do to look too interested, but he was attractive – even if he did support the wrong team. She dropped her eyelashes and returned his smile.
Ellie	What can I get you?
Narrator	The question hung in the air for a second, and the electricity flowed between them.
Man	I can give you something much better than the stuff they sell here, a real thirst quencher.
Narrator	Ellie put her head on one side and frowned a little.
Ellie	I doubt it, we have one of the best selections of drinks in Liverpool* here, all the usuals and lots more beside. I think you'll be satisfied.
Narrator	Flirting with the customers was part of her job, and the customer appeared to be lapping it up.
Man	Not nearly as satisfied as you will be if you take up my offer. Do you want to drink and never want anything else ever again, because it is *so* good?
Ellie	*(Still flirting)* What could be *so* very good? Champagne? I've drunk the very best and gone back for more. Or good old-fashioned tea – the cup that revives?
Narrator	She went down her mental list of drinks, alcoholic and non-alcoholic, smiling as she did so, but was soon stopped in her tracks as the man said,

Man   Water!

Ellie   *(Disbelieving)* Water?

Man   *(Firmly)* Water. Living water. You'll never be thirsty again.

Narrator   Ellie stopped flirting.

Ellie   What on earth are you talking about? I know they have water bars in France and one restaurant in London offers a water tasting to make sure your drink is compatible with your meal – but water is water, a novelty, nothing really special.

Man   My water is. It heals; it springs up within you; it rushes out to satisfy others. Will you drink it?

Narrator   Ellie took an involuntary step backwards.

Ellie   Who are you?

Man   Why don't you go and get your husband and we'll talk more?

Ellie   *(Abruptly)* I'm not married.

Man   Not now, perhaps, but how many relationships have you had? Five, and now this current one?

Narrator   Something akin to fear passed over Ellie's face and she stepped away from the man.

Ellie   How did you know that? Who have you been talking to?

Narrator   The man smiled and Ellie realised he'd spoken to no one. Her tone altered and became rougher.

Ellie   What are you – psychic?

Man   No, but I believe in God.

Ellie   A Jesus Creep! You go to church? *(The man nods)* I don't have time to go there, and anyway the likes of me would hardly be welcome!

Narrator   She could hardly believe she was saying these things, but the man smiled.

Man   The time is coming when you — and your friends — will realise that God can be worshipped in any place, in church, at home, up a mountain, or even in the River Bar.*

Narrator   Before Ellie could reply, the man's friends burst noisily into the pub, but stopped when they realised he was talking to the barmaid, and that might lead to trouble, given their football allegiance.

They tried to hustle him out, wondering why he had become involved with her. Ellie took advantage of the distraction and melted away behind the bar, but she was too excited to fade into the background and she talked excitedly to her work-mates:

Ellie   You see that man over there? Go over and talk to him! See what he tells you — he must by psychic — he could tell me all about myself. I think he's special . . .

Narrator   Her voice died away as the noise in the bar escalated as more and more people arrived. But the bar staff still found time to wander over to the man's table to clear the glasses and to talk to him. *(Ellie quietly disappears)*

Before long, their scepticism disappeared under a barrage of questions and his replies. He listened and he talked. He smiled and bantered and touched their hearts and they didn't want him to go. So he hung around a while longer and met the needs of their hearts as he talked of his Father in heaven and the love God had for them.

And they believed.